INVISIBLE SCARS

ECHOES OF PAIN, SPARKS OF HEALING

PALAK KATARIA

*TO MY FUTURE SELF, MAY THESE POEMS
GUIDE AND INSPIRE.*

Contents

Contents

Preface

The poem within these pages navigate the intricate landscape of the human experience, where beauty and darkness entwine. The collection is a testament to that persistence, a collection of the human capacity to find solace in the brokeness. Through free verse and Imagery, I invite you to step into the fragile world of these poems, I hope you find solace in the words, a reflection of your struggles and triumphs. I extend my deepest gratitude to my parents and my English teacher whose guidance helped shape this collection.

MAY THE RHYTHM OF HOPE, IN RESILIENCE'S HEARTBEAT, ECHO THROUGH THESE PAGES.

1. The Melancholic Muse

Deep inside a wounded soul
Lies the nostalgic and weird hall
Some thoughts run wild
Ghosts of memories never died.
I'm so tired and weak
One moment- trails are waiting for me
One moment- free from every pain
O mother! Buy me candies again
I want to go back to my happy days
Where I could laugh and play.
Today, I'm standing at the shore
And the waves makes it loud
Every damn step feels like a struggle
Everyday seems like a jigsaw puzzle.
A new chapter can still form
apart from the haunted road.

"HER HEART, A HEAVY ROSE, WEIGHED DOWN BY LIFE'S
THORNS, YET STILL, IT'S BEAUTY UNFOLDS."
- SYLVIA PLATH

2. Veils Of Uncertainity

Life unfolds like a painters brush
Each stroke deliberate, each colour lush.
With brushes dipped in hues bold
And some stories yet to be told.
Each sunrise paints a new vow
A canvas of hope, life unlocks
Through the labyrinth of dreams we roam,
seeking meaning, finding our home.
In quiet corners, shadows play
Where uncertainty finds its way.
In the joyful fields or skies of blue,
Moment change, in each possible way.
Life's shadow dancing across the land,
Life's journey shaped by concealed hand.
Amidst the turbulence, hope fly high,
Guiding hearts through darkest array.
In the masterpiece of years gone by.
In the masterpiece, where compassion lie.

*"THE VEIL OF UNCERTAINTY IS LIFTED, AND THE
TRUTH, LIKE A DAWN, BREAKS SLOWLY OVER THE
SOUL."*
- OSCAR WILDE

• 4 •

3. Grief's Ocean

Grief's ocean has no mercy,
no shore to escape the pain.
It floods my days with sorrow,
my night with torment.
I search for a lighthouse, a ray of hope,
To lead me through the void of light.
But the waves pull back,
leaving only the scars.
Grief's ocean, vast and wide and deep,
where waves of pain crash.
Cascades of anguish, floods of grief,
In this sea of memories, I weep.
For grief's ocean is colossal, it's current strong
I Struggle to stay afloat and breathe,
As the oceanic drag, my heart does seize.
But even in melancholy, there's a beauty to find,
Reminding me of what I have lost behind.

"GRIEF'S IS A MOONLESS NIGHT, A DARKNESS THAT HAS
NO END."
- RUMI

4. What If Hallucinations Were Real?

What if pacific is more deeper
on the other side,
Because it's always between Marianas and Philippines.
What if sun shines more brighter
Maybe, grass appears greener too!

Maybe, we're lost on the other side
where, I prefer not to speak.
I am still afraid everyday,
That howl echos
With a terrifying void
Which I really can't avoid.

I'm in a state of crisis
Or maybe it's once again a feeling,
I'll just dismiss
How do I endure this pain, I can't resist.

"WHAT IF THE MADMAN'S HALLUCINATIONS ARE THE
ONLY REALITY."
- FRIEDRICH NIETZSCHE

5. Embers Of Doubt

Who are you afraid to lose?
Your inner self, the nexus of reality?
Or the lies you hide, the silent resonance?
The love that left, or those who stayed?
Or those who lifted you up,
But failed to know you along the way?
Is it your manufactured self?
The shadows of doubt, or the ghosts that haunt your authentic
core?
Or is it you, your unmasked soul,
The one that neglects the beauty of self, a palate of lost passions,
And hunts for unshakeable dedication?

6. Echoes Of Sorrow

Pouring the grief out here
Hoping the better dawn.
I just need to feel okay
But how? I'll think and think.
I drift in and out like waves at shore,
Like a feather in the breeze,
Like an autumn leaf.
My mind is always on the runway,
Yet my body send chills.
I always wonder, when did it start,
Like fast and furious F1 car.
I always find it tough,
For the path I have chosen
As the mist find me frozen.
Today what I see,
Is my mournful smile.
Shifts and blues,
Over and over high.

"SORROWS ECHOES LINGER LONG AFTER THE PAIN HAS
PASSED."
- WILLIAM WORDSWORTH

7. Life's A Poem

Life's a poem,
And I, it's quiet words.
Weaving magic, through the universe,
Centre of calm, though i seem absurd,
I stand against the grain, my spirit expands.
The peom builds me, line by line,
Helps me conquer, help me climb.
Grief once clung, but now it fades,
Embracing solace, in poetic refrains.
Blind you may be, but I have seen,
I know now that I am whole.
I rest my hand,
And free my soul.

"EXISTENCE IS A POEM, CRAFTED BY THE HUMAN
SPIRIT."
- JEAN PAUL-SARTRE

• 14 •

8. The Deep Void

A guilty moom casts its shadow on my window sill
A culture of guilt and guilt's heritage.
I clinch my fists,
And grit my teeth in rage's fire.
My Mind's turmoil,
and expression, I truly can't hold.
Words I use, tainted with venom,
my annoyance trembles
And storm that builds inside
makes my bones ennui.
I lash out once again when all I wanted is to vent and cry,
The tears are full of unspoken phrases and fine mystery each drop
unlocks.

"THE DEEP VOID WITHIN IS THE SOURCE OF OUR
GREATEST FEARS AND DEEPEST DESIRES."
- ALBERT CAMUS

9. Forged In Fire

They say I'm lazy, unaware of my strife,
They know not the struggles that shape my night.
They call me a liar, insensitive to my plight,
They see not the masks that conceal my soul.
They think I'm dumb, oblivious to my mind,
They see not the battles, I triumph through compassions.
They predict my demise, but I'll rise above,
I'll silence their doubts, I'll prove my length.
For I know my strength, forged in the fire,
My benevolence and love, my soul's desire.

"THE FIRE THAT FORGES US ALSO FREES US."
- FRIEDRICH NIETZSCHE

10. Beyond The Miles

Beyond the miles, yet on my mind,
No glimpse of you, my soul entwined.
Through dawn and dusk, I wait for thee
But the abyss of grief has engulfed me deep.
Luna's gentle glow pales beside your beauty,
You ignited joy, enkindled my devasted core.
Your eyes, like stars, bright and clear
Your smiles veiled my dark dreams.
In thoughts of you, I'm lost,
You vanished like a ghost in the night.
A sorrow that remains, a weight that won't subside,
Indelibly imprinted on my mind.

"BEYOND THE MILES, LIES THE MYSTERY OF
EXISTENCE."
- ALBERT CAMUS

• 20 •

11. 'Confractus'

*The prison of my consciousness, an enigmatic entrapment.
I roam endlessly to seek answers day and night.
The walls of my room suffocate me, I search for exit.
I find ways to liberate myself from inner exile,
But anger corrodes the soul,
Bitterness blinds and deafens.
The walls that shelter, now bars of despair.
In love with sadness, a sorrowful echo
Silence, an integral part of my existence.
The grief kills me from within
Endless void of torment.*

*"BROKENNESS IS NOT THE END, BUT A NEW
BEGINNING."
- KIERKEGAARD*

12. Fractured Soul

In the eye of my emotional hurricane,
Mind's cyclone, pulling me under.
And I'm battling my inner voices,
My soul's dark corner, I'm forced to face.
Trauma's ripple effects spread far and wide,
Knive's twisting, in my gut,
Heart's razor, cutting deep,
My bones crack, leaving me wrenched.
Mortal coil, I have transcended fear's limitations,
And then I'll lift the veil of my existence.

"A FRACTURED SOUL CAN BE MENDED WITH THREADS
OF HOPE."
- PABLO NERUDA

13. Triumph Over Turmoil

In shadows deep, my spirit roams,
A warren of silent groans.
In every corner, echoes wail,
a symphony of muted howl.
To face the incubus
one by one,
To see the rising daylight.
With every step, I reclaim my mind,
Leaving the despair far behind.
For in the heart of this thunderstorm,
lies the strength to set me free.
So I'll face the tempest and wild,
with hope as lifejacket and harness braid.
Through the journey may be long and steep,
I'll cross the valleys, conquer and win.
In the depth's of sorrow, find my knight
and rise above the endless nights,
So, I'll operate the twists and the turns,
Knowing each trial, a lesson learned.

"THE BEST WAY OUT IS ALWAYS THROUGH."
- ROBERT FROST

14. A Fading Light

In the depths of my soul, a piece of me lies lost
a beauty that once made my heart aglow- now but a ghost.
In dreams I see his face
but like an illusion, he vanishes,
leaving me with a melancholy that cannot be lifted.
Like autumn leaves, he wilted away
but still, he rests in my memory.
In the tomb of our memories, I'm entombed
A rotten flower, shaken and left to weep.
For this is kept hidden within me
where his voice once whispered
Forever lost, forever longing, my heart remains
A longing reminder of what's been gone.

"IN THE FADING LIGHT, WE CONFRONT MORTALITY'S
MYSTERY."
- MARTIN HEIDEGGER

• 28 •

15. Echoes In The Velvet Hour

In the corridors of my mind, a secret hall
Hallucinations whispered, ripping my heart apart.
I think I'm dead or may be not
I still hear hollow cries, a haunting murmur.
Ghosts of you visit me in the velvet hours
sinister sightings trap me in the cycle of love and pain.

You the garden and grave,
Where I'll lay my head
and let the shadows be my constant guest.

16. Endless Mysteries

He will never know the depth of my existence,
As it exceeds the limits of his understanding,
A deep and infinte ocean, I am,
For the currents of my soul are pure and wild,
Where the void glimmers with a light he can't define,
In this vast and endless blue, he's a ship without a shore,
Unable to navigate the waves of my acumen,
Where the gloom hides the truths he cannot illuminate,
With mysteries that lie without his gaze,
And the whispers that eludes his ear,
The pressure's high,
He's fighting to keep his head up,
And the oceanic silence of my heart stay veiled from his sight,
In the deepest depths of my emotional ocean,
He's submerged and lost.

"THE SEA OF EMOTIONS IS VAST AND UNPREDICTABLE."
- KHALIL GIBRAN

17. Unlost

Within my hollowed chest,
loneliness resides,
a void that feasts on my pschye.
My heart was once a blooming paradise,
but now blood splits in streams,
as though it were champagne.
In solitude, phantoms of my past speak,
a haunting refrain, forever to last.
I just wander, lost and alone,
through corridors of my inner world,
where shadows play and doubts assemble.
Perhaps in time, the storm will pass,
the soul will revive and warmth will unfold.
New horizons will emerge from heartache,
to find tranquility and love again.

"THE ONLY WISDOM IS KNOWING YOU KNOW
NOTHING."
- SOCRATES

• 34 •

18. The Black Sheep

Amidst a sea of woollen white,
The black sheep wanders, lost in sight.
It stands apart, no herd to join,
It dances alone, beneath the starry loin.
With fur as dark as a moonless eclipse,
A muted luminescence in downy disguise.
It's coat is raven black,
The black sheep moves, both bold and tame.
The world may murmer, whispers of doubt,
Yet it marches on, to a different drum.
It's wool, an unseen veil,
Of mysteries others can't hold.
For in shades where others may quail,
The black sheep shines, it's path clear.
Through rolling meadows and steep cliffs,
The black sheep claims a world it's own.

"I'D RATHER STAND ALONE THAN FIT IN WITH THE
CROWD."
- STEVE JOBS

19. How do I calm my Heart?

How do I calm my heart
when it's always racing when it's on the edge of flight?
And winter's here now
how do I move through the cold
when it feels that it has settled within?
How do I stop this noise in my head
when all I hear is chaos?
How do I breathe
when I am choking on the heavy grief.

How do I raise my voice
When I have grown so numb,
Too afraid to be heard?
How do I hold myself
When I'm falling apart,
The pieces of my puzzle have been shattered,
And I don't even know where to begin?

How can I feel warmth again
When I feel like I'm made of ice?
How do I find peace
When my soul has silenced?
When it's all do or die-
When nothing feels certain anymore?
What is my essence,
When my inner self don't even know if I'm alive anymore.

20. 'Icarus'

WITH WINGS OF WAX, AND VIVID FEATHERS,
REBELLIOUS HEART,
AND UNTAMED SOUL.
ICARUS, SON OF DAEDALUS,
A FATAL FLOW, DREAMT OF WHAT IT MEANS TO BE FREE.
BUT HIS WARNING,
HE DID IGNORE, AND SOARED INTO THE ETHEREAL
LIGHT.
THE SUN'S MAJESTIC RISE, WAX WINGS MELTING LIKE
TEARS.
DOWN, DOWN HE FELL,
BENEATH THE WAVES, INTO THE OCEAN,
A SILENT GRAVE.
FOR IN THE SKIES, OUR SPIRIT FIND,
WHERE FREEDOM'S HORIZON MEETS THE INNER LIGHT.

21. Unsaid

Some spoken, some unspoken
Some freely shared, others confined.
In the grace of shifting emotions,
Words emerge, aptly dressed.

Time's mirror reflecting past,
A gaze that focuses, making whole.
A silent road, dry leaves wilting away,
Sorting memories, raw and unturned.
Through life's turbulent tides,
Guided by inner force, most troubled sleep.
With every way, opposing forces sway,
Shining bright, standing tall, come what may.

"SILENCE IS THE LOUDEST SCREAM."
- SYLVIA PLATH

22. My Mother is a walking Miracle

God's best gift to me is not things but,
my mommy!
O my mother dear!!
O my mother dear!!
He took the beauty of sunset,
The grace of the lord himself,
The anger of high tides,
The calm of a quiet child,
The soul as pure as pearl,
The portrait of strength,
The love as deep as pacific,
The dew drops of laughter,
He made you with so much generosity,
Childhood needs are better known,
My mother's exquisite love I own.

There are treasures on earth,
That made life seem priceless.
But there's nothing that compares to my mother's smile.
You are my sunshine to my dark days,
My laughter bag to my melancholy mood,
My source of enlightenment.
You, My mother moon! receiving as you give great happiness.

O my mother dear!!
O my mother dear!!

23. When I was Younger

When I was younger,
The city was a maze,
And I, it's determined explorer!
Time lingered in lazy cadence, days felt endless,
Night's quiet heartbeat lulled me, tranquil sleep.
When I was younger,
The moments merged into a symphony,
I would ride my bicycle until the day drew to a close.
When I was younger,
There were no chains to bind me -
And I...I danced to the beat of my own drum.
There was a rhythm inside me -
A melody that shifted like the wind.
I was unbothered by the tide of judgements,
Oblivious to how I appeared to the world.

When I was younger,
I would gather with my cousins in backyard,
Where a haven of memories were made.

We played hide-and-seek,
Laughter danced over the slope,
Our hearts full of cheer,
We ran here and there without any fear.
Now seasons have shifted, life changed.
I see that those days of limitless freedom were richer than mere
snapshots of youth;
They were the foundation of who I am.

Existence is a garden,
Water the plants of positivity and prune the weeds of negativity.
The lessons of life,
A sacred trust, Guiding me,
Like a radiant beacon in the night.

24. Echoes of a Broken Melody

Strings that once tranquilized my soul
Now cut me deep
Hands that crafted beauty, now perplexed
Fingers that once danced with frets
Now dry and cold
The guitar, my sonic solace
You took my voice away
The melodies that echoed, now silenced by your absence.

25. Fading Beneath the Veil

She once shone,
Now cold and gray
Enveloped in clouds,
Resplendent allure.
Her beauty lost,
A little lie marred her.
Once cheered,
Now concealed in shadows.
A fleeting dream,
A moments gleam.
Lost in deception's dark,
Cold scheme.

• 50 •

26. Rising from the Ashes

Every ray that pierces my fear's veil,
A fragment of darkness dissolves,
And I prevail.

I summon courage,
Entwining soul and heart,
As each radiant beam reveals a new start.

From ashes, a Phoenix will burst forth,
Reborn, renewed,
With strength that never ends.

27. The Poet's Palette

In mental looms, thoughts entwined,
I enter a realm where dreams harmonize.
Though futures fade and paths seem gray,
In poetry, the heart holds sway.
So question not the worth I find,
In stanzas rich,
In echoes kind.
For in each verse,
A world can bloom,
A legacy that breaks the gloom.

28. Silent Screams

In shadows deep where kindness grows,
A heart once bright now carries woes.
With every hand extended wide,
Compassion shines, but guilt must hide.
A steadfast soul, a beacon bright,
In others' storms, they are the light.
Yet when the echoes fade away,
The weight of choices starts to sway.
For every smile they brought to bear,
A quiet voice of self-doubt, rare.
"Did I do enough? Did I miss a chance?"
In giving depths, a hollow dance.
The world moves on, but they remain,
A guardian cloaked in silent strain.
In acts of love, their spirit bends,
Yet in their solace, the guilt transcends.
So stand in grace, let go the weight,
In every moment, you cultivate.
For though the past may haunt your mind,
In helping others, your heart is kind.

• 56 •

29. Cinquains

"RAINDROP ORCHESTRA"

From the heaven, tumbling through darkness
Raindrops fall, each one unique
Reflecting life and never to depart
Nature's ballet, soft and free
Diaphonous dreams, glimpse of poetry.

"SORROW'S SOLILOQUY"

In darkness, I seach for light
Echoes lost in endless night
Traces of euphoria discarded
In the recesses where heartache lies.

"When the thoughts unravel, memories remain."

In the abyss of emotional agony
Lies the odd and redolent pathway
Some thoughts lost control
Yet relics of memories stayed.

"Whispers of the Woven Soul"

The subtle threads of connection, weave gossamer bonds,
Letters hidden, now unmasked,
Delicate ties that bind, an ethereal tapestry.

"Silent Reverie"

My voice, a whimsical thought,
Gone in a puff of smoke, lost.
I'm the leaf on a deserted tree,
All alone and ignored Can anyone hear me?
Am I known?

"Lost in the haze, searching for a way out."

Although my path is shrouded by unraveled ends
I struggle to find a way to softed the edges
Will I find a crack in the abyss or will I be forever
absorbed in the silent void?

"When the thoughts unravel, memories remain."

In the abyss of emotional agony
Lies the odd and redolent pathway
Some thoughts lost control
Yet relics of memories stayed.

"In the stillness, I find my heart's repose."

The quite torment
Will fade and trouble me no more
I sheathe my poetry, with knife's last cut
As I extinguish the candle of my verse.

"Ember in the Winter's Dark"

My star's ember fades,
Soul has silenced,
Sparkles lost,
Petals fallen and winter's darkness envelope me.

"Weight of winter's chill"

Upon their return,
Summer's light will shine my way.
Will they see me for who I'm or,
Will winter's my heart betray?

"Rest Beyond the Grave"

When I'm gone,
Don't visit my grave.
Stand still, in reverence and depart,
No sorrow, no pain, no shame,
Just silence, like falling rain. Visit me not, I'll stand and dance,
Within your soul, my essence stays.
I yearn for calm, not dance or song,
Let me rest, in my quiet bed.

www.ingramcontent.com/pod-product-compliance
Lightning Source LLC
Chambersburg PA
CBHW021135130726
47988CB00003B/1315